DEER
COLORING BOOK FOR ADULTS

Stress-relief Coloring Book For Grown-ups, Containing 40 Paisley and Henna Deer and Stag Coloring Pages

By
Coloring Books Now

ISBN-13: 978-1539983224
ISBN-10: 1539983226

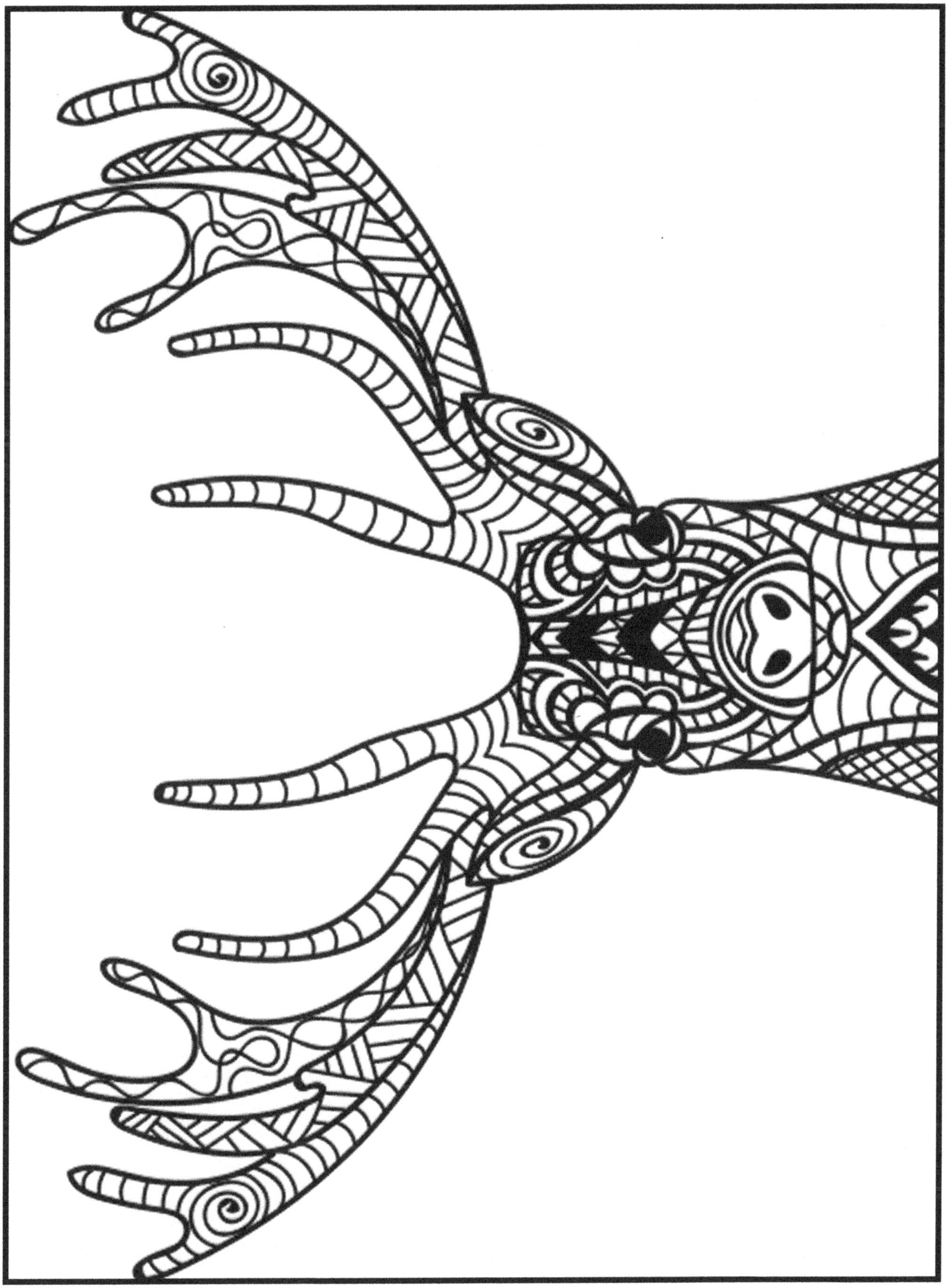

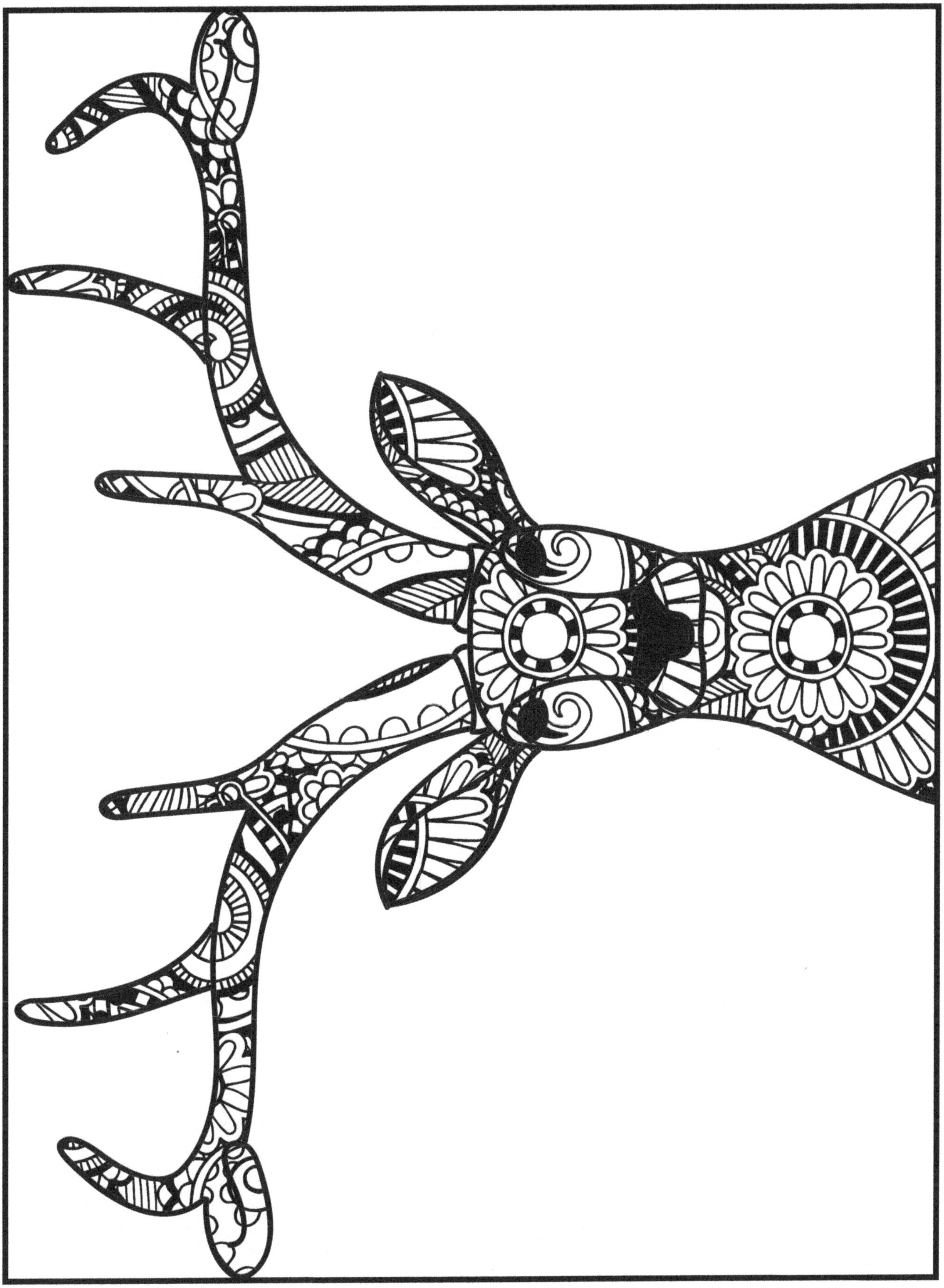

Made in the USA
Monee, IL
13 April 2020

25873217R00046